The SEASON *of* FIRE

Acknowledgements

Several of the poems were first read on radio or television programmes, or were first published in anthologies or magazines. Acknowledgements are due to the producers of The Arts Show (RTE Radio 1), The Pure Drop (RTE 1 television), and the editors of *Aisling, Hot Press, Criterion*, and *On the Counterscarp: Limerick Writing 1961-1991*.

Michael D. Higgins was born in Limerick on 18 April 1941, and reared in Newmarket-on-Fergus, Co. Clare. He studied at University College, Galway, Indiana University and Manchester University, and has for many years lectured in Political Science and Sociology at University College, Galway. In 1992 he became the first recipient of the Seán McBride International Peace Medal of the International Peace Bureau for his work for human rights.

Michael D. Higgins is a Labour TD for Galway West and has twice been Mayor of Galway, and in 1993 he was appointed Minister for the Arts, Culture and the Gaeltacht.

His first collection of poems, *The Betrayal*, which was also illustrated with drawings by Mick Mulcahy, was published in 1990.

Mick Mulcahy was born in Cork in 1952 and graduated from the National College of Art and Design, Dublin, in 1973. He has lived and worked in North-West Africa, Australia, Papua New Guinea, India, Continental Europe and Ireland.

He has had a one-man exhibition in Ireland every year since 1981 as well as several in Queensland, Melbourne, Sydney and Timbuktu. He was a prize-winner in the Oireachtas 1990 Exhibition in Dublin. He has also taken part in Group Exhibitions in Sydney, Queensland, Cagnes-sur-Mer, Germany, Brussels, The Biennial Paris and the Fifth Biennial of Sydney.

The Season *of* Fire

Poems by
Michael D. Higgins

With Drawings by
Mick Mulcahy

BRANDON

First published in 1993 by
Brandon Book Publishers Ltd
Dingle, Co. Kerry, Ireland

Text copyright © Michael D. Higgins 1993
Drawings copyright © Michael Mulcahy 1993

British Library Cataloguing in Publication Data is available for this book.
ISBN 0 86322 164 5

Cover design by The Graphiconies
Internal design and typesetting by Brandon
Printed by Colour Books Ltd, Dublin

Contents

For Sabina, Alice-Mary, Michael Edward, John Peter and Daniel
who have given me so much, but above all for those who would have their story told
and, particularly, in celebration of the right of every story to be shared.

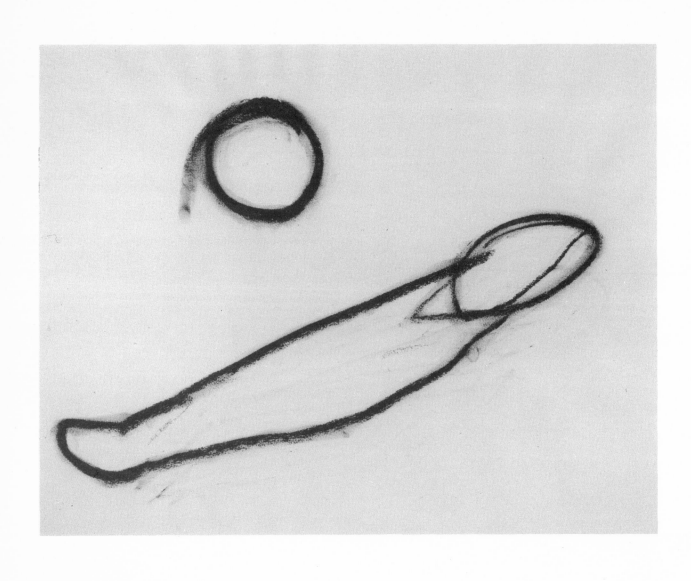

THE SEASON OF FIRE

It is from those barren
moments
that the cloth is woven
of a black suit
of death.

The weaving is not the
work
of a single night or day
but of that thin season
when no fire
lights the darkness.

It is not a season of prayer,
a dry time
when the sap
is not in ebb
but has left.

The death of the loved one
is rehearsed
a thousand times
by lovers
who prepare their black
of the heart
in awful anticipation.

That black is sewn
from a thousand times

of rejection
when the turn of the body
of the loved one
is not read
as the sign of light
in darkness.

The season of prayer
is the time of life
and love,
of look and touch.

And, when the time comes,
it is those moments
that inform the great pain
of a hole in the heart.

The magic of the healing
does not come from
rehearsal
of the weaving of the black
but from an intimacy
of look and touch
in the season of fire.

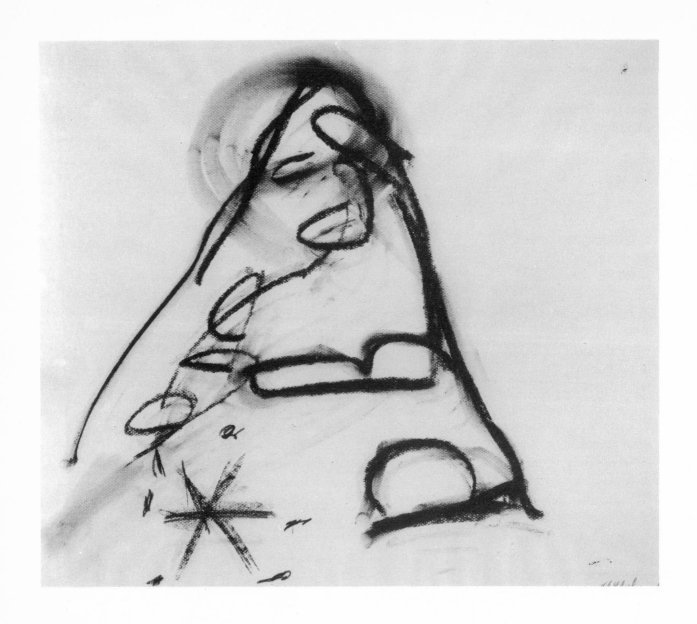

THE MOUNTAIN
(For Alice-Mary)

Pushing out together,
from beneath a caul of dew,
on that morning
I sought to keep a promise
matured with years.
Together we would climb a mountain.
I pushed away my stiffness.
Together we waded lightly through grass.

When we began the ascent
you ran past me,
skipping in the low places,
not wanting
nor heeding my warning.

A smile was sufficient
to displace my irritation
at advice thrown lightly away.

And we rested together
on a plateau.
Together now,
more slowly
we made our way.

When the mist threatened
and the descent began,
there was nobody to whom I could tell my
    own terror.

The words were for myself.
The gaze must never be downwards.
You were a voice I sought
as I struggled to reach again
that place of levelled rock
where I hoped to draw on your strength.

The benefit of touch would be mine,
unlike that time as equals
on our ascent,
and, when I reached it,
you had gone on,
confident.

I trembled.
I was afraid
of the truth that was now
inescapable.
My descent would be alone.
Our journeys together
would end.
Soon, I would not tackle any ascent.

But, standing still,
watching you, loose-limbed and free,
know my daughter
that I would give you
my share of fields
and even those times I saw the sun

break open the leaden lid
of a day,
half-dead with rain,
with a shaft of light.

Oh my daughter,
beyond the mist
and my private terror,
you must sing
for us both.

DRIFTING

In those moments
between sleep and waking,
it is possible
to break the ties
of time and space.

Nearing death,
the word used by those
who lie in beds
is "drifting".

They visit at will
and travel to fairs
and who can say
they cannot travel
to what those left behind
call the future.

Time broken,
space conquered,
drifting;
why should it be confined
to moments stolen
from busy days
or frantic nights
or that place allowed for death?

Glorious body,
vessel of light,

vessel of death,
vessel of life.

And, in those moments
of love
when the heart cries out
or tears come
in wonder
at the explosion
of sense pleasure

or the heart lifts
at the notes of the singer
or it breaks
in a great loss.

Such moments are not messages directed
from some divine power.
Inside the vessel of the person
a miracle occurs.

Drifting,
relegated for rare moments
between
sleep and the tedious day,
for the prelude
to what is called death.

Drifting

is the divine forgotten.
Drifting
is the lost power
of the human.
Drifting
is life stretched
in celebration.

Drifting
is the unknown wine
in the body,
vessel of life.

WHEN MARY DOYLE WENT BLIND

When Mary Doyle went blind,
she saw rabbits playing
and streets full of people
and little dots that frightened her.

The local doctor said it was the blindness
and, anyway, she was old.
It had nothing to do with all the pills
he'd recommended
for her heart, her depression.

Women must listen to doctors.
Relations must not listen to women
who won't listen to doctors.
Relatives must listen to doctors.

The elderly woman, in particular,
must listen to everybody.

Later, she told her daughter
who cared
of what her mother wore
on the night she lay on the bed,
waiting for her to be born.

It was white and had lace
at the neck and sleeves
and she rehearsed her pain
in white and lace

in the old house
on the big bed
with pillows and bolster
all in white.
"And you were beautiful
with a small pink face."
Stretching out her hand,
she feels her daughter's shape
and smiles at all the colours
in her head.

"And when we built the new house,
I fought to have the barn moved back.
There must be space
for flowers," I said,
"lupins, marigolds, Michaelmas daisies,
fuchsias and what we call apple blossom."

Her daughter,
through the window, sees
the tell-tale streaks of brown
that came on the gable
of the old house
in that second season
after the fire went out.
Soot and rain combined
to make a ruin.

Age and loneliness conspired

against Mary Doyle
and, when they were not sufficient,
the pills did it;
and, others too,
women who must listen to doctors,
relatives who must not listen to women
who won't listen to doctors,
men who listen to doctors,
men who listen to women
who listen to doctors;
none of them understood
when Mary Doyle went blind.

THE EYES OF THE LAMB

The silver was the eyes of the lamb
when the scald-crows dived,
the squabble not contrived
as to who would take the prize
of a wedding gift
from a widowed aunt.
The lamb, gone cold, betrays its eyes
as the soot reveals the hearth abandoned
where neighbours come to gather
that which was indiscreetly shown
with untutored pretension.

They are no scald-crows driven by hunger
who gather after
the collapse of a roof
where the tell-tale soot
makes marks on the gable
of the house gone cold.
That which was private and hoarded
is scattered over half a parish,
booty from the destruction
of a neighbour.

The old woman,
summoned to remember,
finds it hard
to explain in a barracks
that once the silver item found
lifted sugar from a bowl

at the stations.

This little bit of what they showed her,
isolated,
was a dagger
to a heart broken a hundred times
from deferred expectations
of recovery
of fate or future.

When fed, the scald-crows fold their wings.
The funeral brings a neighbour's sighs,
moments moral in a barren place
where the lamb must lose its eyes
before the blood is cold
and the abandoned house
the last slivers of hoarded
old decency.

SCUD

On a night when Sky
brought news of Scud and Patriot,
the rattle of rain,
before a long frost
they blamed on Chernobyl,
was heavy on the glass.
In Galway's suburbs,
the slow fog rose
from back-boiler houses
where mantelpieces showed
the newly discovered greetings
of Valentine's Day.

As the rain poured down
on our double glazing,
the bombs were falling
for the hundred and fiftieth time,
with precision,
on target-rich Baghdad.

In our lambing season,
the blood of children spattered
the shelter
where women held the one
that lost a partner
of a tough time
where a leader thought
that to be a cock for a day
was better

than to be a chicken for a week
when faced with an enemy
intoxicated
with the oil
torn from beneath
the flesh of sand.

A sick cow, hundreds of years ago,
scuttered the word
into existence,

Scud,
that breaks the darkness
of the desert night,
the uncontrolled act or word
defined
the scut of our childhood.

Sunday Ceremonies in Clare, 1958

From the moment
of the beguiling words,
assisted with a promise
not to be taken seriously,
to the discovery
of a secret place
of hazel,
floored with damp mosses
and threaded only with an occasional
briar,
it was unstoppable.

The stretch of limbs
among the thorns
brought shrieks of pain,
defeated
by the pleasure
of the pounding
when it came,
all over in a moment.

Nor was there any lingering
as the betraying foliage
was dusted
from the crumpled clothes
that carried
the secret
of this roadside shrine,
a secret made

between the morning pitch and toss
behind the alley
and the encounter
with Sunday afternoon snores,
disturbed only
by a score on the radio
from Croke Park,
this miracle
occurred.

Later, passing the spot
on one's way to benediction,
no guilt
assaulted the senses,
rather
a throbbing recall of memory.

But, when the monstrance rose
above the heads
and wonder came
as to whether
that yawn not stifled
would lock your jaw
forever
at a sacrilege,
the black clouds threatened.

Returning home
the thought rankled,

as the place was passed
where the miracle of discovery
took place,
all rain and mud
and rotting leaves.
No shrine intact.

It would take courage
to decide
that true belief
does not require
a choice between
the shrines
of differing magic.

In Croke Park,
life was easier.
Dublin defeated Derry.

THE MAN WHO KEPT HIMSELF NICE

Face masked with the inside information
of countless cumann encounters
and the cunning
of a cute secretaryship
that ensured the placement
of a large family,
the delivery of collections
of a dusty Sunday,
he had earned the right,
in the evening of a life,
to feel
complacent.

There were no rages in his life
except for that time
in the school yard
the children found two condoms
they thought were balloons.
The disgust lasted
for a full week
and ruined the Sunday roast.

"That kind of thing
might be
what you would expect
from the Black and Tans,"
he'd said
and, when a pupil piped,
"Sir,

weren't they before rubber?"
his fury could no longer be controlled.

"When they lower me down,"
he told them,
"I will be wearing a habit
that tells the world,
even when I'm dead,
that I stood against
all that kind of thing."

At his stage of life,
there was still excitement
in a meeting
with a Minister,
a Cardinal,
even a Pope.

"Keep yourself nice, Winnie,"
Beckett had written
and, God knows,
he had a lot
to answer for.
He'd kept himself nice.

"I've kept myself nice,"
he roared.
"I've believed,"
and the tears came

and they were glad
when the bell rang
and they could run into the yard,
leaving him alone,
the man who kept himself nice.

THE HYMN OF THE MAGPIE

The magpie is a peasant bird,
vulgar,
hard,
with gaudy, bright
colours,
beautiful.

A life of stealing
is revealed
in baubles,
all gathered for their shining
loveliness.

We are magpies,
condemned to be despised,
gatherers of lovely bits
of knowledge,
no purity left,
no elegant
isolated nest
reared us.

We are the birds of the loud screech,
one for bad luck,
two for good luck.
They count us
the vulgar
of the streets,
noisy with our gaudy knowledge

and we can never be
elegant birds,
classy,
with a single refined note.

But there are times
when the light shines
on our bright feathers.
In those moments,
we are beautiful.

THE PETREL AND THE HERON

The petrel
is persistent
in the picking,
jabbing,
stopping only
for the sudden gobble.

The heron stands
still,
an enigma
on the reedy
rock
that the unknowing,
the unwary visit.
Its food
is certain in
the stillness.

The pick of the typewriter
mines words,
the word processor demands
endless feeding, of the
practical
regurgitated
business.

Apart the poet waits
gaze enigmatic,
solitary.

The waiting is rewarded
with the dream that's certain
in the stillness.

A shared space on changing sand
forces no violent supremacy,
rather encourages
a mutual sympathy
for the life
that feeds
from the recurring tide.

The petrel in the
picking and jabbing
stops only
for the sudden gobble.

THE TOUCH 1
(For John Peter)

I had almost made the five decades
when, lying down,
I asked you
to touch my forehead
with your soft hand.
You, just past that first decade
which began with your sister
saying
she loved the feel of you
as a baby,
stretched out your hand.

And, if that touch should ever be
rejected,
could I forgive myself?
And, if it be but
corrupted
by a stranger,
would I not kill for you,
my son of the soft hand?
And, knowing that
I could never bring myself
to kill
another living thing,
would I not hate
and kill
that need,
even in my own head,
that sought your soft hand?

In the delirium of fear,
I have rehearsed these things
that evaporate
in the magic light
of your love.

And if I tremble at your
soft hand,
know that it is in fear
of some temporary invader
of the private space
where our love must always
live.

THE TOUCH 2

On a dark night,
walking down an old road
canopied with hazel,
made treacherous with briars,
you, my red scarved sister,
held my hand.
And, today, I tremble still
in memory of this act
of intimacy that,
at a distance, I might now,
unconvincingly, call love.

I welcomed it
and grew warm
from a strange experience.
At night, I'd curved my body
towards the warm shape
of those who loved and cared.

These acts of touch are burned
in my mind
but, in a dark realm, there lives
another memory
of the stranger,
who told us of water
where we could swim.
We, reared far from the sea,
trusted him
when he said it did not matter

if he watched us
strip away our child's clothes.

And when we stopped
and rejected
his invitation
I still froze
not for an evening
but a lifetime
and all the magic potions
of the Gods
I tried to end my fear
but, in the end,
the patience required of those who loved
became an unbearable pain
and, through tears,
I came to live again,
reach out my hand;
but, I still tremble,
even at the touch
of love.

THE CURRACH

The currach strains to the full
in the low trough
between the unpredictable
mountain that is the wave,
not disentangled
but making a new shape.

The fantasy is revealed
in the white-knuckled joint
that terrifies
in its belief of another life
beyond the predictable
wave.

It is the flimsy base of skin
alone,
well tarred with pitched illusion,
that skims the space
from trough through foam
to the slap
of inescapable fear.

To pull with one hand
is a gesture
of the heroic,
man-made and defiant.
The stillness of the sea
supports the illusion,
allows the fantasy,

for those are the terms
of the old game played
between
the known terror
of life
and the unknown thrill
of the trough
where the currach knows
its fantasy
and survives.

THE PICNIC

I have taken my basket of language
to a quiet place.
I stretch out my rug
on the grass
I remember
as a child.
I note,
even in their disorder,
how well they've travelled
in their sealed containers,
my words.
Looking at their variety,
as a cloud passes,
I remember
I've savoured them all before.

As I contemplate
the meaning
of "al fresco"
the clouds close in
and I remember
I am not hungry
anymore.
That hunger from another season
of the senses
was a fantasy
destroyed
by effort
at re-creation.

MESSAGE TO A POET WHO FOUND MAGIC
(For Brendan Kennelly)

Oh, Poet, who found the marvel
in the simple things,
my heart lifts for you
who has won the freedom
of releasing from within
embraces
I have sought and offered
in public and vulgar places.

The resonance of your chuckle
and the quiet peace
behind the glance
reveal the barrel tapped
and the celebration
of the door thrown open
in the House of Magic;
but, I want to confess,
be forgiven,
for that tyranny of head
that often defeats
the impulse of the heart.

It is not any simple envy,
rather the curse of memory,
that intervenes
to remind me
that utility
has been scraped too deeply
on my bones.

The straightening of the back
left late,
the eyes not free
to see the sparks
of the flight
to the realms of the heart
where you will live
forever.

THE MINISTER'S BLACK CAR

"Still, children.
Stand in line.
Quiet, children.
Be ready when it comes,
the Minister's black car."

Sister Gabrielle is excited.
She hasn't slept a wink.
God forgive her,
she couldn't concentrate at Mass,
thinking of it all,
the new extension,
the opening and
the Minister's black car

Pulling herself together
she tells them again,
"Be ready
Clap when it comes.
Clap when you see it, just
clap, children, clap for
the Minister's black car."

Suddenly she sees it.
"Clap, children, clap.
It's here.
Clap for the Minister's black car."

The Minister's leaving her car.

"Clap, children,
for the Minister leaving her car.
The Minister's smiling at you, children.
Clap, children, clap
for the Minister's lovely teeth."

The Minister's going inside.
"Clap, children, clap."
The Minister's eating a biscuit.
"Clap, children, clap."
Sister Gabrielle is overcome,
her big day.
The Minister's coming towards her.
"You're Sister Gabrielle.
I've heard so much about you."
The children clap for Sister Gabrielle.

Gabrielle's passing out.
"Where are the toilets, Sister?"
she hears in a daze.
"The Minister's going to the toilet,"
she screams.
"Clap, children, clap.
The Minister's spending a penny."

The Minister's car is purring.
The children are lined outside.
"Quiet, children.
Stand in line.

Cheer, children,
Remember, not only when you see her,
not only after she closes her door,
not only after she smiles at me,
until you see the dust.
Cheer, children.
Clap, children, clap
for the Minister's black car."

An Irish Architect Reflects on His Success

Smoothed, shaved and with a hint of purple,
mouth firm and wry-lipped with success,
hair silvered, lovingly jowled,
dentures secure, finger-tips touching
and fat,
a partner.

Half-spectacles perched on a shining nose
for being seen,
he corrects his own intonation,
beautiful tones, perfectly adjusted,
right amount of bass
he talks of contracts
that are a challenge.

Credit card dangling,
his instrument
of purchase,
flaunted
in company that cannot refuse,
even if it intimidates
with its youth.

In days before he went pink
he wore a beard,
was seen
in Wellingtons and mud,
on special days a hard hat
and armfuls of drawings

for he,
they said,
had a lovely touch.

He did not choose to go pink.
It crept over him
like success
and, in that mad transition,
he traded in
his beard
for a bow-tie
that was meant to suggest
maturity
with just a hint
of eccentricity.

He did not get where he is today
from foundations of boardroom lunches,
by making a virtue
of dirt or clients
and his raucous laugh gives way
to a most attractive wheeze
as memories fill his eyes with water,
or is it gin? Who cares?
Flesh of face making no vulgar movement
but now gently rocking itself
across the lovely dimples of middle years.

When he was young he was known

for his good eye
and clean lines.
In kitchens he'd shared moments with couples
who even talked of extensions,
first dissipations of love
and madness of youth.

Staring into the distance, he recalls
the moment of success.
"Pink & Partners" he'd put on his plate
and everyone wanted him.
"Why have anybody else," they said,
"when you can have Pink?"

At Christmas, in bistros, they even sang
a song for him
that he grew to love.
"I once was green but now I'm pink,"
and they humoured him
when the truth no longer could be denied
that he'd gone purple.

It came in flashes
that frightened him
as friends
surreptitiously
talked of heart
but, in the end,
it was a satisfaction

to know
that, when he took his slide-rule home
for the last time
from Pink & Partners,
he'd changed the colour
of his profession
and his universe
for an even greater success,
transition,
special appointment
to God
for renovation
of low-cost housing
for poorer classes
in Heaven.
It was a new beginning;
in time, he thought,
he'd get to tackle
the Mansions.
He gave a long sigh,
why not,
at his success.

FOXTROT IN SAN SALVADOR

In the Camino Royale,
at the edge of the pool,
they are dancing the foxtrot
in full dress,
keeping the show on the road.

The violins
are not weeping
in sympathy
with the blood red leaves
of the bougainvillea tree.

The chlorinated water
shimmers,
carrying,
occasionally,
the shadows of the gloved waiters
whose brown fingers never
touch the cocktails.
Their white gloves
caress the crystal waist
of each glass until
the explosion
rocks the pylon.

The darkness babble
is of irritation
under the candelabras come
to a resounding

cheer
that is backed
by the cheerful monotone
of the standby
generator.

At the edge of the *favella*,
young boys are running
for cover
in a river
of mutually terrified
brown faces.

The shots ring out
and my heart follows them.
Shadows,
the jeeps roar
in the distance.

From the pool
comes the sound
of a polonaise.

_____

Favella: suburban slum

BLACK TUESDAY
(For Norma Elena)

On that black Tuesday,
I saw you
move from the edge of the crowd
where Daniel was speaking
to the *militantes.*
For some, his words were lost.
Enrico had left the night before.
Sitting, head in hand,
his guitar between his legs,
he gave me his only other
possession,
a Juventad Sandinista copy,
shared with Rosario,
his girl;
and he wrote,
"For my Irish friends
in bad times
but asking them to remember
just causes
must, in the end, succeed."

And, when we exchanged an *abrazo,*
your eyes filled with tears
and the dark mahogany of your hair
fell around your face
and the frame that the Gods built
around the lungs
that sang in July, nineteen seventy-nine,
as the last Somoza flew out,

shook and trembled.

But then,
on that black Tuesday,
you were strong.
Walking away, your head was high,
decorated with its band
of red and black;
for you knew there is no going back
and you will sing again,
Nicaragua, Nicaraguita,
when those with blood on their hands,
sheltering behind the lace gloves
of La Donna Violetta Barros de Chamorro,
have gone.
You were no voice for hire.
The campesinos knew your soul.
Abroad, it will be singing.
Norma Elena,
you will come home.

Militantes: the party activists of the FSLN
Abrazo: an embrace

THE STORYTELLER
(For Tom Murphy)

That first man who stood
on a stone
did not grope his way
through the forest
of coy images.
He allowed no requirements
of resonance
to delay his shout
of wonder.

It was passion
that pushed him
past the cowed crowd
of the curious,
beaten into expectation
of necessary ritual.

And, when he gripped them
with his silences,
they felt a tremor
and the stir of blood,
a jet of urine,
all made bearable
with a long sigh.

The coming out,
the going in
of the story
followed no rules

written by clerks.
There were no preparatory flourishes
for what was wonderful.

From that moment
they knew
the origin of magic
and the word
from a man
who took the risk,
defied the rules and,
standing on a stone,
made a story.
They said, unlike the seers,
he was like God
but made them all divine.

St Joseph Blacked from Construction Industry Federation, Bethlehem. All Judea Shocked.

When the scroll was found, they said
it was not just another alternative text.
It was a piece of subversive
slander
and even blasphemous;
but they could not keep it quiet,
the monk who broke the story said.
It was his duty as the son
of a tradesman himself.

It all began in Bethlehem
about a simple manger,
ordered at short notice,
and a simple renovation
of a stable.

Oh, Joseph sang as he sawed the wood
and morticed in the planks
for his little Arab son,
nor did it tax his skill
to fix the stable door.

And when the shepherds came
they stood in wonderment
at the Child
but also at the job
completed
within three days
but, much more wondrous strange,

within the promised time.

They ran and told their friends
who left their flocks
and all through Judea the rumour ran;
a man in Bethlehem
had made a manger,
renovated a stable
within the promised time.
The miracle had been witnessed
by three wise clients from the East.
It's everywhere.
A builder has been found
who keeps his word.

They raged and rent their robes
at the Temple where the builders met,
adjacent to the moneylenders.
"It must be stopped," they shouted.
"It's time to contact Herod
and remind him
who put him where he is."

When Joseph heard the news
his eyes just filled with tears.
He knelt beside his manger,
made in simple deal
and, as his fingers traced the joints,
his son just smiled.

"My son, you'll never be a builder,"
Joseph said,
"for you will tell the truth
and I will free you from the burden
of a daily broken promise
and, from this moment on, I will never
go again to the Temple
to meet the Construction Federation
of Bethlehem."

"Former Chairman resigns."
"Shepherds admit to hallucinations."
"Wise men admit to taking hash."
"Stables renovated by experts."
"Mangers constructed to latest designs."
The Temple press was busy.

And, at the manger, Joseph laughed
for he knew his son
would never need to ask
how his father lost his trade,
was blacked
by the Construction Industry Federation
of Bethlehem.

And, when the scroll was read,
it was reported on to Rome
where it was decided
the scandal was so great

that it was better
to hide the scroll again
in the unfinished crypt
of St Peter's,
himself
a more reliable
stonemason
than Joseph
who, after all,
was a chippie
who could not be trusted
never to keep his word.

PROTESTANTS

It was not the simple act
of nailing the articles
to the church door that did it
nor was it the raving of one man,
even in dissent,
at being told
that God was not available
except through His secretaries
who alone know
his intimacies.

It was the kneeling.
It was the moaning.
It was the mediators.
It was the flowers.
It was the gifts.

And, when it was all done,
they stood up straight
and sang it out.
No flowers, no gifts,
the lungs alone
filled the space.

Nor was there any bowing.
The straight spine would serve them well
in boardrooms and schools,
in trenches and the mess.

Nor did they ever bend
to polish a shoe.
What servants left undone
was matter for the eyes
of those whose backs
were straight.

Brogues and cavalry twill,
moustaches like outposts
on Everest,
tweeds and leather elbows,
pipes and Morris Minors
and, for a while,
they all stood tall
in the Republic
where others bent and knelt
and moaned the mediated prayers.

A straight back brings a cold stare
and it was odd never to see
straight into the eyes
or wonder about the soul
of the many whose backs were bent
in the Republic
of the straight and bent.

Beyond the straight and bent,
there lived in gay abandon
the half-stooped and the crooked,

the broken and the lost.
It was their raucous tongues
that broke the spell
on the frozen ground
between the armies
of straightened backs and bended knees.
They had an older song to sing.

THE PARISH OF SIGHS

The gunpowder blue-black clouds
that stretch behind
the sentinel trees
reveal
a battleground from which
have fled
all the young
and the able,
leaving
abandoned,
in this place of silver
pools
and ever more threatening
darkness,
the quiet keen of loss.

The doors, newly secured
by a bolt rusted from lack of use,
betray
a loss of trust
in strangers
who might have been,
in another time
marked by fear
and grief,
made welcome.

At fifty,
the shutters went

up on the face
of the woman
whose last child had left.
It would take much more
than the snap of a blind's
release
to make her smile again;
more,
an excavation
to that time
when her laugh covered
half the townland
from which her children
were torn
with more pain
than their coming
demanded.

In the parish of sighs
the doors were newly
locked,
the paper scanned
for deaths
that grow more frequent
and the question
could no longer be
postponed
of when one's own turn
would come.

The necessary
preparation
for that moment
defeats
the day distractions
of a temporary
cheerfulness
and, at evening,
time hangs heavy
in the parish of sighs.

STAFF MEETING

Feda O'Donnell's buses
are waiting
to travel north,
bringing home the washing
and the hungry
survivors of cheese and potatoes
at one-ninety-five.

At the Staff Meeting,
no one talks
of Feda O'Donnell's buses.
They are concerned
that nobody is coming
on Fridays
to lectures, seminars and tutorials.

The weekend cannot be recovered
for books and notes.
The washing and Feda O'Donnell's buses
have stolen our scholars.
Between white-faced Monday
and Thursday's drawn visage,
scholarship skulks
at lectures, seminars and tutorials.

MIGRATION SEMINAR
(*For Valdo Pons*)

The migrant on his bicycle
in Stanleyville, he heard,
stopped at every corner
in wonder.
His notes generated
a chapter
in the book of the white
scholar
who hired him.

In the seminar,
the ageing professor
spoke slowly
to those who, unlike him,
had not yet been given a tribe
for dissection.

The migrant in the academy
does not wonder.
He fears
he has not read enough,
he does not belong,
no elegant references,
he has not borrowed enough,
acquired credit
from the dead tomes
of founding fathers
of British anthropology.

It is not enough to know
the suitcase world,
the hole in the heart
on a wet afternoon
at a railway station,
the stark greyness of Euston,
the sad Friday evening songs,
the assembly for Sunday papers
read over pints of mild and bitter.

In the seminar rooms, it is
the economic models,
analysis of social factors
that make the professor nod
and, even if, in moments after sherry,
the professor talked of better days
in Africa
or tried to play the drums he heard
in what the whites had called Rhodesia
before the natives
decided they'd had enough
of British anthropology,
he was reminded
that, in the university,
there was no place
for nature music.

At the interview, they said
they'd never had one really like him.

One from a family
of migrants
who stayed among them, family migrants
listening to the leaden ball
demolish all around them.
"You're most unusual," they said.
"You must at seminar one day
tell us about your people."
Escape had brought him here.
He thought he could belong,
a migrant in the academy.

The migrant on his bicycle
became an appendix.
The migrant in the academy
grew sad.
He filled his suitcase with a hundred papers
and took them home
where others listened,
at a distance,
to the thoughts without drums
at second hand
gathered in Africa
by a professor
of British anthropology.

And the discovery came,
much too late,
that he should have had the courage

to demand the right
that space be made
at the seminar
for his own story,
for nature music.

THE DEATH OF MARY DOYLE

She knew that there was thunder
in the air
from the sulphur
she had come to know.
All day she had waited
for a visitor
to read the letter
from her daughter,
the nun,
who had written
earlier that week
from Africa.

Moving her hand along the handle
of her stick,
she sighs at all the stories
she has ready
of the older people
who had gone before her,
farmed these stony acres.

She talked too much,
she thought,
in recent times
and then it all came clear
in silence.
She would go to the barn.
She loved it there
where all seemed warm

and intimate too.
Taking her stick,
she stumbles
out the door
and pushes through the yard,
undisturbed
by green pools
of urine
and dung,
damp under her feet.

And it is the dryness
of the barn,
its thousand smells,
a shrine
that welcomes her.
In recent years she'd come to know
a strange fire that sparks
from the embers,
not lit from desire
but intimacies
stored
from days and nights
spent here
in better times
and all the laughter that filled this place.

Leaning towards the bin,
the smell of meal moulded

stirs the memory
and pictures come
of hens and cheerful chatter,
the stickiness of new-born calves,
gelatine heeled,
unsteady,
needing the pull of both hands
to stand

wobbling,
waiting for the rack lick
of a cow's tongue
that was, with laughter,
invoked
to describe the quiff
of her first son's hair.

The colours of all the feathers
in a hundred nests
warm her heart
that fills
as she tried to feel
the rounded shapes,
finger poked for eggs
in the bride years of her marriage.
Slowly rising, the warmth
moves from her fingers
through her body,
shapeless from the birth

of seven children.

Exploding through her head,
the thousand pieces,
gathered
in sense memory,
overwhelm.

She falls towards the crib
where the wood,
polished
by the neck of an itchy cow,
is marble smooth and warm
but offers no grip.

Lying tumbled in the rank hay,
she laughs
and still the colours come
of gold and amber,
of green gone brown.
She had it all.

The limber shoot
was browned by a season
that ran its course.
That rich gold head of grain
would break the stalk
in times of storm
or broken weather;

but, more often,
the stooking and the binding
intervened
between the time of fields
and the predictable
breaking
of the threshing.

She was an old sheaf
cut loose from binding,
all seed taken,
only the dried stalks
ready
for the bedding
of all the life
that heated with their breath
this barn.

They found her
pitched forward
among the hay
and screamed
when they saw the youth
of the smile
that covered all her face.
Her stick abandoned,
she held in each hand
straw and feathers.
They would have to clean her up

for the laying-out.

They did not speak
to each other
or the neighbours
of where they found her
and, at the laying-out,
a holy woman
claimed
she heard a crowd
of angels
come to bring her up,
inevitably,
to Heaven.

It was not angels that sang her home
but cows and calves
and ducks and hens
and they gave her colours
for her head
and voices too
and smiles
and smells
and the touch of love.

Not long after,
they decided
that it was better
to knock the barn.

It was upsetting,
particularly
to the holy woman
who said
it held memories
that disturbed her
of that day
when Mary Doyle
went out to the barn
to die.

THE DELIVERY
(*For Daniel*)

I have delivered my children
to school
in the half-grey light.
Always,
the half-grey light
reminds me
of anxious arrivals,
temporary releases.
Hurried half kisses,
furtively offered,
must be sufficient
for that time
of the offering up.

Leaving,
I question my complicity.
No blind faith any longer
moves me.
I am the deliverer
of what were my children
to the Chapel of Fear,
for sacrifice.
I weep full tears,
Alone.

THE COLLECTING

As my eyes peel the playground
I am distracted by sounds that are chaotic
celebrations of release.
The harness of satchels
is being tossed
with a disrespect
hard earned.

The bag, discarded,
is placed in perspective
by an involuntary kick
from a stranger
who had not invested it
with the intimacies
of welts and warm shoulders.
It is the peopled yard
that attracts
the backward glance.

The classrooms, abandoned,
linger in empty silence
until morning
when the breath of authority
will, again, define
their arbitrary purpose.

Their long shadow
captures the first words,
"I've a pile of homework."

We drive on homewards
with the wedge of school between us.

The Search

THE BLACKNESS

Sweating and turning in the bed,
he thought of lost papers.
"Neurosis," they said
and always it would end
with a question
as to whether he'd lost the small photo
of a man, all neck and hat
and a grey glimpse
of a broken spirit
that passed for face.

The blackness was there
that frightened him
and he rushed for rescue
in the suggestion
that all life
is a new beginning.

But, when his turn came
for middle years,
the photo tormented him
as did the unknowing
who said,
"You're the image of your father."

Even his mother
would withdraw
that phrase.
His father

devalued
everything he touched.

The escape made necessary
took its full price,
absorbing all thought
and feeling, too,
to reach the certainty
of knowing
the past had been
defeated.
It was no celebration
of present time.

The parched plant
betrays its shrunken roots
with burned leaves.
The feelings long suppressed
left him half broken
from desperate excess
at compensation.
The miracle was in the coming
to his hospital bed
of one who, in a moment
of that despair,
saw the suffering soul
beneath the wit.

Closing his eyes, he remembered

her coming with a potted plant
for his window.
As if on air, she moved,
lightness in a room
of darkness.

And when she had left
he felt her hope
lingering
in the room
of darkness
that dispelled the gloom
of what he'd brought upon
himself.

And can a miracle be repeated
in later years
when the cursed blackness threatens,
the photo returns
to haunt?

With strength, a temporary victory only
is possible.
He would look for love again
in the eyes of his children
where who knows, or when,
rejection would ever surface.

And he would hold again their mother's hand,

lost love
found again by way
of those small faces.

The shadow would lift
if he could leap
past that photo of the forties
to five years earlier still
to when that other snap,
as they called it then,
showed a fresh-faced man with hope,
a woman falsely modest
in a leather coat,
both not defeated yet by life
or that shadow that had come
to haunt their child,
half-grown man.

Each life might yet begin
its story
with a moment chosen
before the blackness
shown in an old photo
from the forties.

The image can defeat
the heart filled with love.
It is when the heart's gone empty
that blackness strikes.

He'd fill his heart with joy,
with tears,
with love
or pain.

There would never be,
if he could manage it,
a vacant space
where the cursed darkness
came to lodge
but for a fleeting
moment
in the longer moment
of life.

A Hopeless Case

Sitting in a corner,
they looked at him
weeping.
The consultant said
he had not spoken
for years
but often wept.

He was an interesting case,
a great "speaker"
in his day,
until he snapped,
the consultant said.

At an early stage
in his treatment,
they read him all his speeches back.
It was his worst time.
His weeping gave way to rage,
the consultant said.

And it provoked a fit
when he broke into verse.
They thought
they'd cracked it.
"In the age of denim,
between leather and brushed cotton..."
he began,
but stopped.

In shock they heard him say,
"Nothing happened."
The flood of tears came,
the consultant said.

"A hopeless case;
we can't even make out
for whom he's weeping.
Is it for himself?
Is it for his life?
Is it for the family?
Is it for some great cause?
We'll never know
for sure,
but I have a hunch
it's something to do with language
and the speeches.
It's very hard to know
what they're about
when they snap,"
the consultant said.

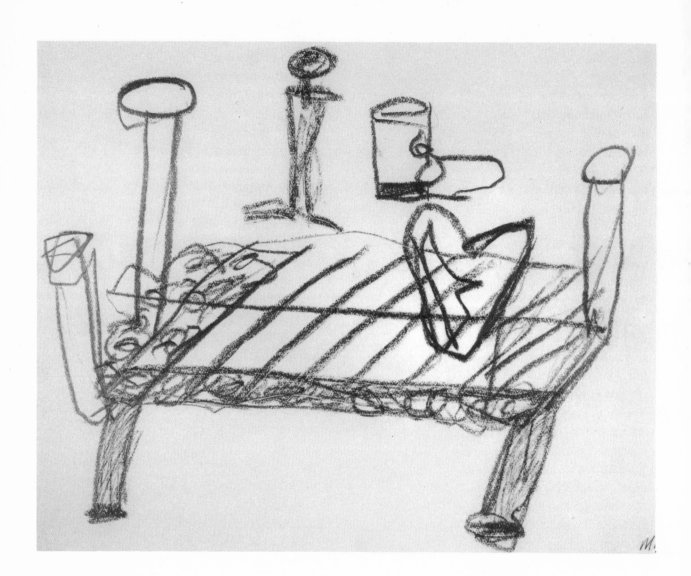

BROTHERS

When we set out together to find
our new home,
I suspect
we cared less
for the broken heart of our mother
who had let us go
than for the wonder
of the journey
in a black Ford Eight
through fields
at twilight.

It is that wonder
that brings me back
to the age of five,
not any great grief
I should have felt
or tears I should have shed.

And then, we were
together,
a source of curiosity,
a legacy from tragedy
that had given a childless pair,
an uncle and an aunt,
two instant children,
brothers
so alike
we could be twins.

That's what they said.
We did not find
the bonding
of such words
a burden.

We stood together in photographs.
Our teeth defined
a hidden difference
and, on our city visits,
both wearing boots
for the lasting,
not shoes,
that we were told by our mother
were the mark
of civilisation
and the city,
our communion suits, chosen
for next year's wear,
the sleeves
played with our knuckles,
another country sign
that made her sad.

At night, we shared a prayer
in a room
demoted from a parlour
to being the sleeping place
of aunt and child,

of uncle and child,
the parlour now the space
of what had once been
a four-poster bed,
a sofa and sister bed,
a well-sprung inheritance of iron,
replete with tick and bolster.
We learned those country words,
the rites of night
and intimacy.

Their shaking preceding our prayers,
"Matthew, Mark, Luke and John,
God bless this bed that I lie on."
Evangelists.
I learned the word
and thought of bells
and books
and quills
and long grey beards.

I placed them nightly
on the missing poles
of the bed, mutilated
without its postered canopy,
acquired from the scattering
of a half-great local house.

And little things were made

for the little men
who would be one day sure
to be a great help
when needed in hayfields
and the bog
or in the wet brown drills
of tillage.

You were better at all these
practical tests
of strength
and judgement, too.
For me, the image of escape
distracted
from the tasks of place.
The books I loved
were instruments
for the breaking of the bars
and a run
towards the light
and a new life
back
in the city.

At times, on the bar of a bike,
I vowed
to bring you
where I presumed
you wished to go.

It was through pain
I realised
that our journeys
would be separate,
alone,
requiring different skills.

And I sought my brother
in a hundred others
for whom
my heart warmed
at shared
hopes
and fears.

Every embrace a compensation
for the lost moments
of feelings
buried beneath
the boulders
of other expectations
of duty
and respectability,
of fear
and dust
and sweat
and a life reduced
to rehearsal
for the decency in death

that was the legacy
of our family.

Back from the tomb,
Christ saw brothers
everywhere.
The stone rolled back,
he never returned
home
but embraced every stranger,
brothers all
in the light
out of the dark.

KATIE'S SONG

It is a story buried
beneath the clay of past
intimacies,
a time sealed,
made safe from disturbance
and a label that warns
of the danger in opening
the moulding jar
of memory.

And yet, I see her,
legs stout,
apart,
trying to snatch private time
for woman business,
for us the source
of wonderment
but, much more,
the threat and origin
of an averted gaze
that could never be
corrected.

Oh Katie, I remember
when your writing carried a flourish
and the lightness returned
to your fingers
as you smiled the magic
on the schoolbooks you covered,

satchelled ambassadors
twixt home and school,
our steps to the future.
Your fantasy
compensation
for a life
of lesser things.
Oh Katie, I would sing your song
if now I could recover
more
than your moments
of intimacy
and fantasy,
two threads that did not make
alone
the garment of your life.

On a sometime Sunday,
I recall
your playing with magic words.
You dressed yourself
with such unusual care
that the violence of my question
as to where you might be going
did not dislodge you from your dream.
You were not going to any haggard
that afternoon.
You were, instead, intent on strolling
in a pleasure garden

and you told us you had an appointment.
We, whose thoughtless demands
defined
your every action,
could not understand.

And, when you died,
after calling us for an hour,
your summons from the fields
not heeded
not perceived,
your anxious tones
faded,
alone,
at a distance
from children not your own
moved to an unbearable anxiety.

Oh Katie, I am making my way
along a lane of hazel.
I am stretching
for the fire of the senses
that will being me back
to where I can stand still and shiver
and weep
at all the love
you earned
never paid
by a child afraid,

in iceberg times,
to throw his arms around
the plump frame
of the maker
of his bread
and magic.

QUESTIONS WITHOUT ANSWERS

Thinking
in private,
overcome
by the loneliness of pain,
a man hauling a bucket
of concrete
on a nearby site
seems
suddenly
very significant.

What is it
that I am leaving?
The sudden beauty
of the known,
dull and predictable,
assaults all the senses.
Every blade of grass
a miracle,
newly invested
with a tapestried
wonder.

Thinking,
on that bad night in hospital,
that I might die,
it was a question
I feared.
After the decay of flesh,

could there be
a holding on
of hope against that fear
that, after all the pain,
the time spent
will be alone,
infinite
loneliness.

The rock-wedged flower
of the Burren
exists alone.
The pain reduces life
to being
a piece of meat,
mechanical system,
dislodged of hope,
abused.

Not in charge of any choice
of faith,
in stillness,
the lost opportunities for softness
haunt
and give way to a glimmer
of light
in a small corner
of the despairing dark.
The miracle

is in this moment
of the fundamental question.

Are we the children
of some great cosmic
conflict?
Are we the children
of some great unfinished
dream?
Are we the flimsy pieces
of some great unfinished
symmetry?
There could be no answers.

The child's grief will pass.
The spouse's loss will last
for a longer season,
resonant
of a thousand shared
moments.

There is no evasion
of the concentration
on the question required
for answer
in this moment
alone.

Again it comes,

the suggestion
that the answer is in a question
but the frightened mind
flies back and forth
in terror.
What if the question had no answer
or had an answer
for which I am too late?

Now, it is necessary,
in desperation,
to throw all cerebral pretence
aside
and, in humility,
ask
if one could be sure
of some old connection
following
between the unavoidable
rot
of the body
and the resilient
spirit.

Black and barren,
a bucket of concrete
lifted by a man
begins the story
of a new day

on a site next door,
a story whose tedious finish
will succeed me.
I need a miracle now
to save
my own belief
in a renewable
season of fire.

Turning from the window,
I weep for the futility
of questions without answers.
I must have this space
but, in all the smaller
gestures,
I will look,
in whatever time is allowed,
for magic moments
where little statements
between questions and answers are made,
bright coals
worth the raking,
embers of the season of fire
where my miracle will come.

My terror shared,
my fear
bespeaks
a life of senses

beyond
a speck of dust
and, more than that,
the spark that flickers
will become a flame
shared
in collective concerns,
set alight
from a fire source
older than the sun.
The answer
is in the flame collective.
No longer am I alone
and dawn breaks.

On the long night
of my lonely pain,
my miracle,
born in a moment of terror,
blazes
with the gift of seeing
the beauty
of the ordinary.
I am making my way
home.
I hear the words,
"Take care."

TOES
(For Michael Edward)

Watching the sole of your foot
curled,
I see in the perfection
of its shape
a possibility
of belief
that no random collision
of fact
gave me the feelings
I encounter
as I gaze on those small toes
in perfect shape
as you sleep.

No piece of chance
or probability
can explain
my feeling
that overflows,
my son,
my love,
my frail hope
of belief
recovered.

The Journey

BEYOND THE I

Beyond the I
there is a golden space,
a shared place,
not in any sky,
no fantasy
escape.

And getting there
requires
a frightening journey
through the gaze
of the other.

To see your seed
in every child's eye
and feel that every wrinkle
in a worn hand
was your own skin
gone dry
requires a journey
that few may take.

For, once begun,
the terrifying gaze
requires
the journey be complete.
That look
in all the children's eyes
will start a fire

in the heart
that no private words
or gesture
of limb or lip
can quench.

In the first stumbling
you may be helped
by allies
for a part
of that journey
through the first challenge.

But alone
you must make it through
the fire
where the death of the I
is required.
to the blinding light
where, unsteady and weak,
you appear
bent,
near broken.

But all hands combine
in the space of light
and beckon
all human,
not one I

but occupants of a shared space where,
at last,
all hearts can beat
together,
that space
of no difference
beyond the I
where life no longer defies
death.

And a great unity
brings peace
with all creation,
defiled
no longer
by the I.

TAKE CARE

In the journey to the light,
the dark moments
should not threaten.
Belief
requires
that you hold steady.
Bend, if you will,
with the wind.
The tree is your teacher,
roots at once
more firm
from experience
in the soil
made fragile.

Your gentle dew will come
and a stirring
of power
to go on
towards the space
of sharing.

In the misery of the I,
in rage,
it is easy to cry out
against all others
but to weaken
is to die
in the misery of knowing

the journey abandoned
towards the sharing
of all human hope
and cries
is the loss
of all we know
of the divine
reclaimed
for our shared
humanity.
Hold firm.
Take care.
Come home
together.

THE NOOK

Back through an old bunch of rhythms,
as between briars battered
to reveal a space
of new growth
inviting invasion
of its emptiness,
I lash my way.

That journey back from reason
follows no known path.
There are only lurking spaces
on the spiral,
defying the arrogance
of Descartes,
of Pascal,
of Racine,
of Aquinas,
of Aristotle.

The gods of secure reason
have to be beaten aside,
illusions discarded,
to reach that place,
a womb recovered.

It is a space made
for decay
but also the hidden life
beneath the dying leaves.

Deprived of light,
the thin branches affirm
the struggle.

It is a place of soft mosses
encased with thorns,
a sanctuary
made with purpose,
achieved.

No random shape
of uncontrolled branches,
it invites
in its uncertainty.

TRIBUTE TO A FRIEND

The moth, now weak,
that flung its wings
with passion
against the evening lamp,
lingers with feeble
gestures
on a sill,
discarded,
waiting for its last
faint beat of death.

The pine cone,
seal broken,
lies splayed
revealing,
in its separated wings
the power of fire.

Life soiled,
family broken
anxious made
by threatening time,
desperate,
driven from deep despair
to seek a solitary solace,
he remembers
he has embraced the white waist
of a hundred toilet bowls
and prayed before the ceramic object,

pressing his mouth in violent
humiliation.
Shaking with emotion, he has prayed
and begged of any god
for help.
Just to end this awful state
he is willing
to believe in anything.
Shaking and faint, he leans
on the door
of his sanctuary
of bolts and privacy.

Off-stage, the terror strikes.
He wipes the white water from red eyes
and, straightening,
leaves the shrine
to make another entrance.

No lingering moth
or pine cone cracked,
not divine either
but human,
he remembers,
on safe deposit
in the heart,
are lodged
moral moments,
precious

in their stored energy:
a gaze from a child's eyes,
a cooling hand on a tormented forehead,
an embrace.
He is ready.

Eyes closed, he begins,
vulnerable,
taut
as strings waiting
for the touch of the bow,
sliding back
to a time before fire
and on beyond the sun
in silence.
He curtseys
before the breaking
of the applause.
Together,
words have been broken,
magic discovered
and, later, after tears,
he knows
that life beckons
to the light
where moth and cone and poet
are one.

Unity Recovered

On a night when sleep was slow
in coming,
in the shadow of the Albert Hall,
the gift came
as the body curved,
no longer in search of return
to the womb.

Ratio sought the common fluid
along the spiral
of mystery,
uniting at last with Eros,
and celebrated
their lost unity.

Choosing from the richly coloured blankets
of myth
that warmed in a long sleep.

The story of the soul
carried in the million threads
more truly
infinite,
not bounded
male or female,
the spirit of a new age
renewed.

Technos discarded

after the liberation
at last,
free
and at one.
The journey was over
in ecstasy.

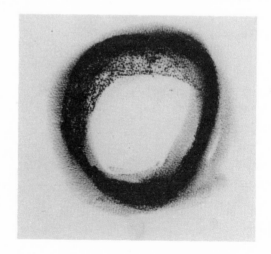